The Bicycle:
Vehicle for a Small Planet

Marcia D. Lowe

Worldwatch Paper 90
September 1989

Table of Contents

Introduction

I n a world so transformed by the automobile that whole land-scapes and lifestyles bear its imprint, a significant fact goes unnoticed. While societies the world over define transportation in terms of engine power, the greatest share of personal transport needs is met by human power.

From the 10-speeds of Boston to the black roadsters of Beijing, the world's 800 million bicycles outnumber cars by two to one—and each year bike production outpaces automobile manufacturing by three to one. Bicycles in Asia alone transport more people than do all of the world's autos.[1]

In developing countries—where urban workers cycle to their jobs and rural dwellers pedal two- and three-wheelers piled high with loads of goods—pedal power is an important part of national economies and the only alternative to walking that many people can afford. In industrial countries, bicycles are a practical supplement to motorized transport.

Meanwhile, a steady rise in the amount of driving in the world's major urban areas is pushing congestion and air pollution to intolera-ble levels. The by-products of gasoline combustion—air pollution in cities, acid rain, and global climate change—point to the need for an alternative to automobile-centered transportation.

Widespread use of mass transit, though a worthwhile goal at any stage of economic development, is difficult to achieve. Third World governments unable to provide adequate public transit for the bulk

I would like to thank Andy Clarke, Michael Replogle, Ken Hughes, Charles Komanoff, Ralph Hirsch, Setty Pendakur, Ellen Fletcher, and several of my colleagues at the Worldwatch Institute for their helpful comments on an earlier manuscript; any remaining errors are my responsibility. Special thanks to Peter Skillern for hours of lively debate on the relative virtues of cycling and driving.

6 of their populations can better afford investments in bicycle transportation. In industrial countries—where official efforts to encourage use of mass transit are often rejected by people who are accustomed to individualized transport—the bicycle is the only vehicle that addresses car-induced urban problems while providing convenient, private travel.

Cycling has covered a great deal of ground since the invention of the chain-driven bicycle in the late nineteenth century. Bicycles quickly became commonplace for the industrial working class and were introduced in colonial societies. Today pedal power brings mobility to the remotest villages and densest metropolises of the globe, but a post-war boom in auto use has nearly obscured the utility and ubiquity of the bicycle. Only China and a few Western European nations collect transportation data that count bicycles among forms of transport.[2]

Fewer than 1 percent of the Third World population can afford an automobile, but many developing countries have imported a mind-set along with their few cars. Western-trained engineers and car-driving elites skew transport decisions toward the motorized sector. The result is that millions are left on foot, with limited access to jobs, schools, markets, and vital services.[3]

A few countries do encourage bicycling in their transportation strategies. Public policy in China—and to a lesser extent in Japan—began to foster cycle commuting when limited access to motor vehicles left people with little choice. Today several industrial countries promote bicycling as an alternative to over-reliance on automobiles.

Public policy can facilitate cycling in a number of ways. By making ordinary streets safe for bicycles and providing a network of cycleways—separate cycle paths, bike lanes on streets, and wide shoulders to accommodate cyclists on major roads—physical improvements can give cyclists and drivers equal access to as many destinations as possible. Providing bicycle parking at mass transit

> "Pedal power brings mobility to the remotest
> villages and densest metropolises,
> but a post-war boom in auto use has nearly
> obscured the bicycle's utility and ubiquity."

stations—an option known as "bike and ride"—may be the most
cost-effective way for authorities to conserve fuel and reduce vehicle
emissions.[4]

Governments can further promote a cycling environment by making
auto users bear more of the full costs of driving. Removing hidden
benefits such as subsidized parking and revising tax structures to
reflect road investments and pollution costs would treat petroleum,
clean air, and land as the scarce goods they have become.

A pro-bicycle stance is not necessarily anti-automobile. The
Netherlands, the most bicycle-friendly of all industrial countries,
has—along with a high level of public transit service—the Western
world's highest densities of both cycleways and cars. Indeed, maxi-
mizing the use of bicycling and mass transit could curb the steep
growth in driving before urban air becomes unbreathable and rush
hour traffic grinds to a standstill.[5]

Broad support for cycling is not likely to come without action by
individuals, advocacy groups, and other institutions. As societies
gradually see the potential role of bicycling, an alternative scenario
comes into view: a diverse transport system that does not harm the
environment, demands little from the economy, and gives crucial
mobility to millions of people. Getting there will require going
beyond entrenched transport solutions to fulfill the potential role of
the bicycle—the vehicle of the future.

The Silent Majority

In China, traffic noise means the whirring of bicycle wheels and tin-
kling of bells. Throughout South Asia, pedal vehicles rigged with
trailers, baskets, and load platforms haul everything from passengers to squealing pigs and sacks of rice. Nicaraguan health workers
cycle through the countryside to reach remote patients, and Kenyan
dairy farmers make their milk deliveries by bike. Australian
"posties" pedal through town with their mail bags, European com-

muters often cycle to their workplaces, and thousands of bicycle couriers zip past stopped cars in North America's gridlocked urban centers.

Most of the world's bicycles are in Asia. China alone has roughly 300 million—more than one for every four people, or almost one for every two city residents. Traffic monitors at an intersection in the northern industrial city of Tianjin once counted more than 50,000 bicycles pass in one hour.[6]

Chinese commuters have little choice but to make the most of their bikes; nationwide, only 1 person in 74,000 owns an automobile. Bicycles are also popular because, like cars in industrial countries, they offer the luxury of individual mobility and door-to-door travel, without detours or extra stops for other passengers. When the same trip takes equal time by cycle or mass transit, most Chinese commuters prefer to bike.[7]

The last emperor of the Qing dynasty, Pu Yi, pedaled around the Forbidden City as a child, long before ordinary citizens could afford to buy bicycles. In the seven decades hence, and particularly since the sixties, the Middle Kingdom has become known as the "Bicycle Kingdom." During the last 10 years, rising incomes have been matched by rising bicycle purchases, and the country's fleet has nearly tripled. Domestic bike sales in 1987 reached 35 million—surpassing total worldwide automobile sales.[8]

Elsewhere in Asia, bicycles often make up two-thirds of the vehicles on city streets during rush hour. Many Asian urban transit systems are enhanced by pedal-powered "paratransit," consisting of three-wheeled vehicles for hire—variously called rickshaws, trishaws, pedicabs, and becaks—in which a driver transports one or more passengers. These resourceful adaptations of the bicycle do much the same work automobiles do elsewhere. Cycle rickshaws are the taxis of Asia, and heavy-duty tricycles, hauling up to half-ton loads, are its light trucks. In Bangladesh, trishaws alone transport more tonnage than all motor vehicles combined.[9]

> "Cycle rickshaws are the taxis of Asia, and heavy-duty tricycles, hauling up to half-ton loads, are its light trucks."

The rest of the developing world lags far behind in bicycle transportation. In much of Africa and even more widely in Latin America, the prestige and power of auto ownership has made governments ignore pedal power and led citizens to scorn the bicycle as a vehicle for the poor. Before some African nations became independent, colonial administrations built urban bicycle lanes or paths, but most have deteriorated or been abandoned in the past three decades. And many African women do not ride bicycles for reasons of propriety or religion or because of encumbering clothing.[10]

Africa and Latin America lack Asia's widespread domestic bicycle industries. The few bikes available are often of poor quality, spare parts are scarce, and maintenance skills inadequate. In Nicaragua, for instance, an estimated 80 percent of the bicycle fleet is in poor repair.[11]

Despite these constraints, the bicycle's utility and the lack of other options have led to more intensive cycling in some African settings—even if it means splicing together worn-out brake cables or filling a punctured inner tube with sand. Parts of Zimbabwe, Burkina Faso, Ghana, and a few other countries have heavy bicycle use.[12]

Latin America too has its cycling pockets, where the vehicle's practicality transcends its low social status. In Colombia's capital, Bogotá, the city's largest bakery traded in most of its trucks for 900 space-saving delivery trikes that now bring goods to over 60,000 local shops. Nicaragua became perhaps the first Latin American government to promote cycling actively, pledging in 1987 to supplant its war-ravaged transport sector with some 50,000 bicycles, some purchased by the government and some donated by other nations.[13]

Several heavily polluted areas in Eastern Europe and the Soviet Union have encouraged a revival of bicycling as part of their environmental strategies. The Lithuanian city of Siauliai launched the Soviets' first comprehensive cycling program in 1979. A new bike path system and extensive parking facilities have helped raise bicycle use in the city. In small Hungarian cities, roughly half of all journeys to work are by bike.[14]

Industrial countries have a surprising number of bicycles per person, considering how few are typically found on most city streets. (See Table 1.) Many industrial nations have two or three times as many bikes per person as their Asian counterparts. But where people have access to automobiles, bicycle ownership does not necessarily mean bicycle use. One in 4 Britons has a bicycle, yet only 1 transport trip out of 33 is made by bike. In the United States only 1 of 40 bikes is used for commuting; most of the rest are ridden for fitness, sport, or play, or are collecting dust in the basement.[15]

A comparison of bicycle and automobile ownership illustrates each country's reliance on bicycles for actual transport. The United States has more than seven times as many bicycles per person as India, but because 1 out of every 2 Americans owns an automobile—compared with 1 out of 500 Indians—bicycles play a much more modest role in the U.S. transportation system. (See Table 2.)[16]

Western Europeans are the industrial world's heaviest bicycle users. In several countries—among them Denmark, West Germany, and the Netherlands—bike owners outnumber nonowners. Pro-bicycle planning in the last twenty years (rather than conducive climate or flat terrain, as is often assumed) distinguishes Europe's truly "bicycle friendly" countries. The Netherlands and Denmark lead this group, with bicycle travel making up 20 to 30 percent of all urban trips—up to half in some towns. In several European countries, 10 to 55 percent of railway patrons in suburbs and smaller towns arrive at the station by bicycle. Traffic jams and air pollution in the past decade have spurred authorities in Switzerland, West Germany, and Austria to encourage more bicycle use. Cyclists in the United Kingdom, Belgium, France, and southern European countries, by contrast, still enjoy little support.[17]

Many automobile-saturated cities of North America and Australia have all but abandoned the bicycle for the automobile. The growth

Table 1. Bicycles per Person in Selected Countries, circa 1985

Country	Bicycles Per Person
Netherlands	.79
West Germany	.74
Japan[1]	.49
United States[1]	.42
Australia[1]	.42
China[1]	.27
Mexico	.16
South Korea	.15
India	.06
Malawi	.01

[1] 1988

Sources: Worldwatch Institute, based on United Nations, *Bicycles and Components: A Pilot Survey of Opportunities for Trade Among Developing Countries* (Geneva: International Trade Center UNCTAD/GATT, 1985); and other sources.

of suburbs has sent jobs, homes, and services sprawling over long distances that inhibit cycling, as well as mass transit. Many major cities are largely bicycle-proof, their roadways and parking facilities designed with only motor vehicles in mind. While Australia has a set of planning and design guidelines for bicycle transportation, state and local governments often ignore them, lacking a sense of commitment to transport options other than the automobile. Several North American cities explicitly emphasize safety for cycle commuters—including Seattle, Calgary, and some university towns—but these are exceptions.[18]

Society also has a growing number of bicycle options, as engineers continually bring out new models designed to be lighter, more rugged, more efficient—even protected from the weather.

12   Table 2. Bicycles and Automobiles in Selected Countries,
circa 1985

Country	Bicycles	Autos	Cycle/ Auto Ratio
	(millions)	(millions)	
China[1]	300.0	1.2	250.0
India	45.0	1.5	30.0
South Korea	6.0	.3	20.0
Egypt	1.5	.5	3.0
Mexico	12.0	4.8	2.5
Netherlands	11.0	4.9	2.2
Japan[1]	60.0	30.7	2.0
West Germany	45.0	26.0	1.7
Argentina	4.5	3.4	1.3
Tanzania	.5	.5	1.0
Australia[1]	6.8	7.1	1.0
United States[1]	103.0	139.0	.7

[1] 1988

Sources: Worldwatch Institute, based on Motor Vehicle Manufacturers Association, *Facts and Figures* (Detroit, Mich.: various editions); MVMA, various private communications; United Nations, *Bicycles and Components: A Pilot Survey of Opportunities for Trade Among Developing Countries* (Geneva: International Trade Center UNCTAD/GATT, 1985); *Japan Cycle Press International*, various editions; and other sources.

Alternatives include rugged, off-road bikes, recumbents, on which the rider reclines while riding, and hand-crank bicycles for the disabled. Tandems allow two persons to combine their muscle power. Folding bicycles enable commuters to stow their vehicles under bus seats or in trunks.[19]

The world is sufficiently equipped—measured by the number of

Table 3. Production of Bicycles and Automobiles, Selected Countries, 1987

Country	Bicycles	Automobiles
	(millions)	
China	41.0	.00[1]
Taiwan	9.9	.20
Japan	7.8	7.89
United States	5.8	7.10
Soviet Union	5.4[2]	1.33
India	5.3	.15
West Germany	2.9	4.37
South Korea	2.6	.79
Brazil	2.5[2]	.68
Italy	1.6	1.71
Poland	1.3[2]	.30
United Kingdom	1.2	1.14
Canada	1.2	.81
Others	10.5	6.54
WORLD TOTAL	99.0	33.01

[1] In 1987 China produced 4,045 automobiles.
[2] 1986 estimate.

Sources: Worldwatch Institute, based on Motor Vehicle Manufacturers Association, *Facts and Figures '89* (Detroit, Mich.: 1989); *Japan Cycle Press*, various editions; and other sources.

vehicles—to let bicycles take on a larger share of the transportation burden. Nearly 100 million bicycles are made each year, three times the number of automobiles. (See Table 3.) Backed by strong domestic demand and growing export markets, major bicycle producers, especially in Asia, are sure to keep expanding their capacity.[20]

The automobile—which has brought industrial society a degree of individual mobility and convenience not known before—has long been considered the vehicle of the future. But countries that have become dependent on the car are paying a terrible price: each year brings a heavier toll from road accidents, air pollution, urban congestion, and oil bills. Today people who choose to drive rather than walk or cycle a short distance do so not merely for convenience, but also to insulate themselves from the harshness of a street ruled by the motor vehicle. The broadening of transport options beyond those that require an engine can help restore the environment and human health—indeed, the very quality of urban life.

Despite improvements in safety, an estimated quarter of a million people worldwide die in automobile accidents each year. Millions more are injured. Developing countries—with fewer automobiles but more pedestrian traffic and no provisions for separating the two—have fatality rates per vehicle mile up to 20 times higher than industrial countries, and road accidents have become a leading cause of death.[21]

Nearly everyone who lives in a large city is exposed to another hazard of the automobile era—air pollution. Cars and other motor vehicles create more air pollution than any other human activity. Gasoline and diesel engines emit almost half of the carbon monoxide, hydrocarbons, and nitrogen oxides that result from all fossil fuel combustion worldwide. Airborne lead, sulfur dioxide, particulates, and many other pollutants—most of them harmful, and some toxic or carcinogenic—also spew out of the tailpipe.[22]

A recent report by the World Health Organization and the United Nations Environment Program estimates that up to half the world's cities have harmful levels of carbon monoxide, and one-third have either marginal or unacceptable concentrations of lead. The study also estimates that up to one-fifth of North American and European urban residents are exposed to excessive levels of nitrogen oxides.[23]

Chemical reactions among these emissions create a pall over
metropolitan areas, aggravating bronchial and lung disorders and
often proving deadly to children, the elderly, and fetuses. The main
ingredient of car-induced smog is ozone. Formed as nitrogen oxides
and hydrocarbons interact with sunlight, ozone—an essential shield
from deadly ultraviolet light when in the stratosphere—is a health
threat at ground level. In 1988, some 96 metropolitan areas in the
United States, home to about half of all the country's residents, failed
to meet ozone safety standards set by the U.S. Environmental
Protection Agency. On particularly hazy days in the world's worst
smog-filled cities—Mexico City, Athens, Budapest, and many others—officials must call temporary driving bans to avert public
health crises.[24]

The seriousness of air pollution in developing countries, the Soviet
Union, and Eastern Europe threatens to rise along with soaring
growth in the size of their automobile fleets. The number of cars in
the Third World, though still minuscule compared with that in
industrial countries, is growing roughly twice as fast. Automobile
fleets in the Soviet Union and Eastern Europe, where passenger car
production has been ignited by growing consumer pressure, grew at
more than twice the world average rate of 3 percent during the first
half of the eighties. Effects on future air quality will be acute, since
controls on auto emissions in many developing countries are virtual-
ly nonexistent, and those in the Soviet Union and Eastern Europe are
frequently inadequate.[25]

Car-induced air pollution does damage far beyond city limits.
Vehicles are a major source—in the United States, the largest
source—of nitrogen oxides and organic compounds that are precur-
sors to ozone. Ozone, believed to reduce soybean, cotton, and other
crop yields by 5 to 10 percent, takes an estimated annual toll of $5
billion on crops in the United States alone. Nitrogen oxides themselves can be chemically transformed in the atmosphere into acid
deposition, known to destroy aquatic life in lakes and streams, and

16   suspected to damage forests throughout Europe and North America.[26]

As serious as these losses are, they pale in comparison to the disruptions that global warming could inflict on the biosphere. Motor vehicles' contribution to worldwide output of carbon dioxide—the greenhouse gas that accounts for roughly half of the warming effect—is estimated at 17 percent. Carbon monoxide contributes indirectly to the warming by slowing the removal of methane and ozone, two minor greenhouse gases, from the lower atmosphere.[27]

Excessive motorization also deepens the oil dependence that is draining national economies. In 1988, U.S. oil imports cost some $26 billion, or more than 20 percent of the country's foreign trade deficit. Many nations' transport sectors account for more than half of their petroleum consumption. In the United States, the share is 63 percent, and in Kenya 91 percent. Even with the recent fall in crude prices, fuel bills are particularly harsh for indebted Third World countries that spend large portions of their foreign exchange earnings on imported oil. In 1985, low-income developing countries (excluding China) spent on average 33 percent of the money earned through merchandise exports on energy imports; many spent more than half.[28]

The oil shocks of the seventies brought home the precarious nature of petroleum as an energy source, exposing car-dependent countries' vulnerability. Today's stable prices and supply have lulled importers into complacency. But as oil demand continues to rise, another oil crisis looms in the nineties.[29]

The world's largest gridlocked cities may run out of momentum before they run out of oil. Traffic in many cases is moving at a pace slower than bicycles, with average road speeds during peak times sometimes down to 8 kilometers per hour. Some police units in European and North American cities—including London, Los Angeles, Victoria, and many others—use bicycles rather than squad cars for patrolling congested urban centers.[30]

In some parts of the Third World, urban gridlock is even worse. **17** Traffic density in Taiwan's capital is 10 times that of congestion-plagued Los Angeles, and work trips take Mexico City commuters up to four hours each day. In Nigeria's capital—which experienced a doubling of its fleet during the oil boom of the seventies—"one quarter of the problem of working on Lagos Island is getting to work," according to one civil servant. "The rest is getting home."[31]

The economic and social costs of congestion, already daunting, are bound to multiply if car commuting trends persist. The Confederation of British Industry warns that traffic congestion costs Britain $24 billion a year—including employee time lost through tardiness, and inflated goods prices resulting from higher distribution costs. The U.S. Federal Highway Administration put the country's loss to traffic jams at $9 billion in 1984. The FHWA expects a fivefold increase in that amount by 2005. Some 50 percent more cars are projected to be on the road then, the typical commuter's 10- or 15-minute delay may stretch to an hour, and roads will likely be congested throughout the day.[32]

To date, planners have typically sought only technological solutions to auto-induced problems. Without support for alternatives to driving, however, these fixes may be inadequate. For example, the catalytic converter that has contributed to impressive reductions in hydrocarbon and carbon monoxide emissions in the United States actually slightly increases the carbon dioxide buildup that contributes to climate change. And while the converter and other technological cures have dramatically reduced pollution from U.S. passenger cars since the early sixties, rapid growth in the vehicle fleet and miles traveled have partially offset this progress.[33]

Similarly, the quest for petroleum alternatives has focused largely on "clean" fuels such as methanol, made from coal or natural gas, and alcohol substitutes distilled from corn and other crops. But methanol contributes to ozone formation and, if derived from coal, to climate change by emitting twice as much carbon dioxide per unit

18 of energy as does gasoline. Using crop-based feedstocks for alternative fuels poses its own environmental side-effects, and a potential conflict with food production.[34]

Nor is building more roads the answer to congestion. Transport planners are finding that constructing new freeways just attracts more cars, as some public transit riders switch to driving and new developments spring up along the new roads. In 1988, a California Department of Transportation study concluded that neither a $61 billion road building program, nor *any* further road building, could solve its traffic problem.[35]

Even if such solutions could work, society is running out of resources to devote to the automobile. Industrial-world cities typically relinquish at least one-third of their land to motor vehicles for roads and parking lots. As former FHWA Administrator Robert Farris said: "We can no longer completely build our way out of the congestion crisis by laying more concrete and asphalt. Time is too short, money is too scarce, and land is often not available."[36]

Third World countries with mounting pressures to house and feed their swelling populations have even less room to spare for private automobiles. Where people and good cropland are concentrated in a relatively small area, as in China, choices are few. For China to pave over as much land per capita as has the United States (about .06 hectares) would mean giving up a total of 64 million hectares—equivalent to more than 40 percent of the country's cropland.[37]

For every person who makes a trip by bicycle instead of by car there is less pollution, less fuel used, and less space taken on the road. Bicycle transportation, rather than replacing all motorized trips, would mainly supplant short automobile trips, precisely those that create the most pollution because a cold engine does not fire efficiently. A shift to bicycles for these trips would therefore yield a disproportionately large benefit. Considering that more than half of all commuting trips in the United States and nearly three-fourths in the

United Kingdom are eight kilometers or less, bicycle commuters could become an important component of an effective clean-air strategy.[38]

For longer trips, linking bicycling with mass transit through improved access to transit stations holds great potential for reducing energy use and air pollutants. According to a 1980 Chicago Area Transportation analysis, bike-and-ride is the most cost-effective way to reduce hydrocarbon and carbon monoxide emissions. Giving cyclists secure parking at transit stations would reduce hydrocarbon emissions at a public cost of $311 per ton, for example, compared with $96,415 a ton for an express park-and-ride service, $214,959 for a feeder bus service, and $3,937 per ton for a commuter rail–carpool matching service. Carbon monoxide reductions would come at similar savings.[39]

In the United States, 33 states included bicycle promotion measures in their plans to implement the Clean Air Act of 1970, and more are expected to do so after the act's 1989 revisions. One such measure is the imposition of "trip reduction ordinances" as in Los Angeles, where major employers must reduce the ratio of motor vehicles to commuting employees. Also in effect in other western cities, these regulations specifically list bicycle parking and employee shower facilities.[40]

In Europe, the Dutch government recently announced a national environmental plan that includes road tolls and tax rebates to expand use of public transit and bicycles. Several Italian cities beset by smog-induced health emergencies and damage to historical structures have prohibited nonessential motor vehicles in their central areas, encouraging drivers to cycle instead.[41]

In the rush to run engines on gasoline substitutes such as corn-based ethanol, decision makers have overlooked a technology that converts food directly into fuel. A cyclist can ride three-and-a-half miles on the calories found in an ear of corn—without any distilling or refining. Bicycles consume less energy per passenger mile than any other form of transport, including walking. (See Table 4.) A 10-mile commute by bicycle requires 350 calories of energy, the amount in one bowl of rice. The same trip in the average American car uses 18,600 calories, or more than half a gallon of gasoline.[42]

A 1980 study in Great Britain calculated that if just 10 percent of car trips under 10 miles were made by bicycle, the country would save 14 million barrels of oil a year, or 2 percent of total consumption. In 1986, a national campaign in the Netherlands encouraged drivers to switch to bicycles for trips within a 5-kilometer radius of home. Policymakers estimated that this would save each motorist at least $400 a year in fuel costs.[43]

A 1983 study of American commuters revealed that just getting to public transit by bicycle instead of by car would save each commuter roughly 150 gallons of gasoline a year. When a motorist who otherwise drives all the way to work switches to bike-and-ride, his or her annual gasoline use drops by some 400 gallons, half the amount consumed by the typical car in a year. At current prices, if 10 percent of the Americans who commute by car switched to bike-and-ride, nearly $1 billion would be shaved off the U.S. oil import bill.[44]

Bicycle transportation also uses space more efficiently than automobile transport. In fact, all other modes, especially mass transit options, can move more people per hour in a lane of a given size than an automobile even at the top of its range. (See Table 5.) Since bicycles offer the same degree of individual mobility as automobiles, replacing short car trips with bicycling could ease congestion without curbing people's freedom to move when and where they choose. Replacing longer car trips with mass transit—especially with cycling as the way to get to the station—would save even more space on roads.[45]

Relief from traffic is something everyone can enjoy, not just drivers who choose to cycle instead. Many cities in the industrial world temporarily close major streets to motorized traffic, in effect turning them into wide cycle and foot paths. In 1983, Mayor Augusto

Table 4. Energy Intensity of Selected Transport Modes, United States, 1984

Mode	Calories per Passenger Mile
Automobile, 1 occupant	1,860
Transit bus	920
Transit rail	885
Walking	100
Bicycling	35

Sources: Mary C. Holcomb et al., *Transportation Energy Data Book: Edition 9* (Oak Ridge, Tenn.: Oak Ridge National Laboratory, 1987); President's Council on Physical Fitness and Sports, private communication, June 23, 1988.

Ramirez Ocampo launched such a program in Bogotá, Colombia, under the slogan "the city for the citizens." Every Sunday morning 56 kilometers of arterial roads are closed to motor traffic and half a million city dwellers take to the streets to cycle, roller skate, or stroll.[46]

Bicycle transportation could help restore balance to people whose daily lives are in many ways governed by the automobile. Philosopher Ivan Illich has concluded that the average American male "spends four of his sixteen waking hours [driving his car] or gathering his resources for it."[47]

The daily battle with traffic congestion, according to a recent University of California study, tends to raise drivers' blood pressure, lower their frustration tolerance, and foster negative moods and aggressive driving. Except when there is no alternative but to ride in the same traffic stream, commuter cyclists benefit both themselves and their employers by being less vulnerable to hypertension, heart attacks, and coronary disease, and arriving at work more alert. The proof that people enjoy cycling to keep fit is in the popularity of sta-

Table 5. Number of Persons per Hour that One Meter-width of Lane Can Carry, Selected Travel Modes

Mode	Operating Speed[1] (kilometers per hour)	Persons[1] (per meter-width of lane per hour)
Auto in mixed traffic	15-25	120-220
motorway	60-70	750
Bicycle	10-14	1,500
Bus in mixed traffic	10-15	2,700
Pedestrian	4	3,600
Suburban railway	45	4,000
Bus in separate busway	35-45	5,200
Surface rapid rail	35	9,000

[1] Ranges adjusted to account for vehicle occupancy and road speed conditions in developing countries.

Source: United Nations, *Transportation Strategies for Human Settlements in Developing Countries* (Nairobi: Center for Human Settlements (Habitat), 1984).

tionary exercise bikes; the irony, however, is that so many people drive to a health club to ride them.[48]

Measured by its benefits both to society and the individual, the bicycle is truly a vehicle for a small planet. "Bicycling is human-scale," writes New York cycling activist Charles Komanoff. "Bicycling remains one of New York City's few robust ecological expressions... a living, breathing alternative to the city's domination by motor vehicles. There is magic in blending with traffic, feeling the wind in one's face, the sheer fact of traversing the city under one's own power."[49]

Most people in the Third World will never sit inside—let alone own—an automobile. Private car travel is the privilege of only a tiny elite, and thinly stretched public budgets cannot provide adequate public transit services for burgeoning populations. Bicycles and their three- and four-wheeled derivatives can enhance people's mobility at little cost, improve access to vital services, and create a wide range of employment opportunities. Yet deeply impoverished countries pour precious export earnings into motorized transportation, ignoring or even subverting human powered options that citizens and governments alike could better afford.

An automobile in developing countries can cost as much as 30 times the annual per capita income—or an estimated 18 to 125 times as much as a basic one-speed bicycle. It is no wonder there are so many persons for every automobile in the developing world. (See Table 6.)[50]

Motorcycle ownership is growing in many countries—usually much faster than car ownership—but is still beyond the means of the majority. Mopeds are increasingly popular in Asian cities and have promise as an intermediate vehicle. Both motorized two-wheelers, however, pose their own pollution problems.[51]

For many people in the developing world, the only affordable alternative to walking is a public bus, and yet even in urban areas buses can be scarce. (See Table 7.) Many Asian, African, and Latin American cities—where the majority of people are dependent on buses—have less than half the coverage of U.S. and European cities, where riders usually have the option of driving anyway. Rural bus service is much worse. Expanding Third World transit systems could easily overwhelm government budgets burdened by crucial needs such as housing, water supply, and sanitation.[52]

Privately run bus companies often play an important role in developing countries, easing the government's transit burden. These services also fall short, however, for lack of equipment and fuel; a

Table 6. Population per Automobile, Selected Countries, 1987

Country	Persons per Automobile
United States	1.8
France	2.6
Japan	4.1
Venezuela	11.4
Malaysia	12.4
Brazil	15.5
Tanzania	44.9[1]
South Korea	50.2
Senegal	88.8
Thailand	94.0
Egypt	123.6
Nigeria	141.0
Ghana	217.0
India	544.4
China	1,074.0[2]

[1] 1985
[2] Refers to all automobiles; population per privately owned automobile was 74,000 in 1988.

Source: Worldwatch Institute, based on Motor Vehicle Manufacturers Association, *Facts and Figures '89* (Detroit, Mich.: 1989).

further obstacle is the high incidence of unpaved or narrow streets.

Moreover, even where bus services are available and reliable, they may not be affordable. In a survey of cyclists in Delhi, 35 percent said they cycle because bus service is inadequate and 43 percent said they cannot afford a bus. In much of the Third World, fully meeting transport needs through mass transit is a worthy, but likely unattainable goal.[53]

"For many people in the developing world, the only affordable alternative to walking is a public bus, yet even in urban areas buses can be scarce."

Particularly in rural areas, therefore, people have little choice but to walk. Rural transport in developing countries consists mainly of moving farm goods and supplies and gathering household necessities such as water and fuel. Families spend an inordinate amount of time gathering fuel and water each day, with women carrying the brunt of this hardship quite literally on their heads. A study in Kenya found that women do 89 percent of all water and firewood gathering for the family. Water collection, probably the most pressing rural transport problem, uses up more than 25 percent of a person's daily energy requirements in some rural African areas. Women and children may spend three to six hours a day fetching water for the household.[54]

25

Across the developing world, farmers typically need to haul loads up to 150 kilograms over moderately long distances. These tasks do not call for a truck or automobile, but they do require some intermediate kind of vehicle. Throughout tropical Africa and parts of Asia, even a "small" load of 30 kilograms becomes a crushing burden when carried on the head, back, or shoulders. Headloading and other forms of human porterage can severely injure the spine, joints, muscles, and internal organs. According to a report in Bangladesh, half of broken necks are incurred from falls while the victims were headloading. Handcarts, pack animals, and pedal vehicles are used to varying degrees in different countries, but even where animal transport is common, headloading and backloading are often the primary means of moving goods.[55]

Field studies conducted by Intermediate Technology Transport, Ltd., a London-based agency that gives technical assistance to local development projects in the Third World, have shown that a bicycle can increase a person's travel capacity (a combination of speed and payload) by at least five times over that of walking. Attaching a trailer to a bicycle allows the rider to comfortably carry up to 200 kilograms—several times the maximum headload.[56]

Nonmotorized transport could greatly reduce the amount of time and human energy wasted in this headloading and footpath econo-

Table 7. Bus Services in Selected Cities, 1985[1]

City	Total Buses	Per 1,000 People
Seoul, South Korea	44,252	4.59
Chicago, United States	29,000	4.33
Karachi, Pakistan[2]	16,822	2.71
Stockholm, Sweden	2,640	1.67
São Paulo, Brazil	24,300	1.53
Helsinki, Finland	1,168	1.50
Mexico City, Mexico	25,050	1.39
Abidjan, Côte d'Ivoire	2,111	1.17
Shanghai, China	7,707	.99
Adelaide, Australia	748	.76
Jakarta, Indonesia	5,635	.70
Amman, Jordan	730	.62
Cairo, Egypt	5,794	.55
Calcutta, India[2]	4,150	.42

[1] All figures include buses run by public and private bus companies.
[2] 1983 data.

Source: World Bank, Urban Transport: A World Bank Policy Study (Washington, D.C.: 1986), and other World Bank documents.

my. Except where cultural mores prohibit their use, these low-cost vehicles could ease in particular the daily ordeal endured by women. Although men in many African countries traditionally do not collect water for the household, they have been shown to do so in some surveys—if it is by some form of transport other than back-loading or headloading.[57]

Engineers are at work on a variety of adaptations of pedal technology for the Third World. The "Oxtrike," originally developed in the seventies by Stuart Wilson at Oxford University, has a large platform for heavy cargo and is sometimes equipped with gears. Several international organizations are working with local authorities in

"Bias against human powered vehicles
is severe in Third World cities,
and even worse in the countryside."

developing countries to design sturdy load-carrying bicycles and **27**
trailers, and improve vehicle designs for the disabled. Job S.
Ebenezer, former director of the Rural Appropriate Technology
Center in Madras, India, represents one of several groups designing
ways to adapt a bicycle to other purposes—powering a paddy
thresher, a peanut sheller, or a water pump—so that it can be easily
adjusted back again for transportation. Inter Pares, a Canadian agency, is redesigning rickshaws originally developed for six-foot
Europeans into lighter, cheaper, and more maneuverable vehicles for
the typical five-foot Bangladeshi.[58]

Bicycles provide a livelihood for many in the Third World's informal
sector—the mass of self-employed entrepreneurs who, operating
with little or no capital, make up 20 to 70 percent of the labor force in
urban areas. Mobile vendors cycle with bundles of newspapers
through Tanzanian towns, bring hot lunches to factory workers in
Sri Lanka, and display fresh bread on their bicycles in Iran.[59]

Cycle rickshaws provide a livelihood for hundreds of thousands of
drivers and their dependents. For landless peasants, rickshaw driving offers a step up. Unnayan, a Calcutta advocacy group, calculated that in 1980 a rickshaw driver earned nearly $300 a year, well
above the average income. Rickshaws in Bangladesh account for
more than half of all passenger trips in the city and employ an estimated 140,000 drivers, owners, builders, and mechanics. Pedal
power is also crucial in goods distribution. Some 5,000 *tricicleros* in
Santo Domingo, capital of the Dominican Republic, use heavy three-
wheelers to circulate much of the city's supply of fresh food, coal,
scrap metal, and various materials for recycling.[60]

Professor V. Setty Pendakur of the University of British Columbia, an
authority on urban transport in South Asia, believes that the social
benefits of pedal powered transit—employment, access, and affordability—far outweigh the disadvantages, mainly the lack of efficien-
cies of scale possible with motorized public transit.[61]

But bias against human powered vehicles is severe in Third World

28   cities, and even worse in the countryside. For decades, national governments have devoted rural funds to building motorable roads, neglecting the fact that almost no rural dwellers have cars or trucks, and motorized public transit rarely reaches them. Study after study has shown that by far the greatest movement of people and goods takes place not on the road system at all, but among farmers' fields and between home and sources of water and fuel. Transportation expert Wilfred Owen has noted that "many miles of roads in poor countries prove more useful for drying beans and peppers than for moving traffic."[62]

Although policymakers could expand transport at little cost by supporting bicycles and other human powered vehicles, they seldom do. City governments are often hostile to rickshaws and similar services, either discouraging them with regulations, fines, and taxes, or wiping them out entirely through bans and confiscations. Dhaka, Bangladesh, recently threatened to phase out rickshaws—despite the fact that they account for more than half of all passenger trips in the city and employ an estimated 140,000 people. In Jakarta, Indonesia, the city has confiscated some 100,000 cycle rickshaws over the past five years and dumped them into the sea—to "reduce traffic congestion." Rickshaws throughout South Asia, and even in some African countries, where they are less common, are also in jeopardy.[63]

Governments typically defend their assaults on rickshaws by declaring them unsafe or inhumane for the drivers. The more likely motive, however, is to clear the streets of vehicles that make the city look poor and backward. According to Pendakur, "The cycle rickshaw provides the highest employment for a given investment and serves the poor efficiently and flexibly, reaching areas not reached by conventional buses. While there is a need to modernize and make the life of the rickshaw puller tolerable, the answer may not lie in costly motorization but in better design of the cycle rickshaw and the streets."[64]

Governments are not the only ones reinforcing discrimination

against human powered vehicles. As Michael Replogle, president of
the U.S.-based Institute for Transportation and Development Policy,
has noted, the World Bank—a principal source of urban transport
funds in the developing world—published a 400-page study of
China's transport sector that fails to even mention the word bicycle.[65]

There are signs, however, that some change is happening at the
grassroots. In 1982, Santo Domingo vendors, with support from private development agencies, formed the Association of Tricicleros.
The association began as a loan fund to help the vendors buy their
own vehicles, eliminating the high rents they had been paying to
owners. Continually pressuring the city's traffic and police depart-
ments to lift unfair restrictions, the association has successfully lob-
bied the municipal government to lower *triciclero* registration fees,
which were formerly higher than those for taxis.[66]

Developments in recent years suggest that human powered vehicles
may yet penetrate official circles. A handful of national governments, lending banks, and other international agencies that have
steadfastly pursued motorization policies are finding their one-track
approach to transportation unsustainable. An example in progress
is an intermediate transport project in Ghana—operating with support from the World Bank.

In 1985, the government in Accra recognized that, after years of supporting motorization, its transport sector was failing to meet the
most basic needs of moving people and goods. With assistance from
the World Bank and advice from Intermediate Technology Transport,
Ghana is now promoting the production and use of bicycle trailers
and handcarts. The bank is also proposing to help Ghana build low-
cost rural roads meant chiefly for nonmotorized vehicles. Sufficient
to serve an occasional truck or car without having to meet stricter
construction standards, the proposed roads would cost about $2,400
per kilometer, or roughly 8 percent of the cost of a conventional rural
road.[67]

Use of human powered vehicles is increasingly common among

30 employees of development agencies, who find they are the best or sometimes only way to reach remote villages. Under some conditions, a jeep that is vulnerable to breakdowns and fuel shortages is more costly and less effective than a fleet of bicycles. Oxfam and UNICEF have purchased bicycles for health workers in Africa, and family planning and other organizations use pedal power to serve their constituencies in several African and Latin American countries.[68]

The Institute for Transportation and Development Policy sends donated bicycles and parts where most needed to improve people's access to services and free the hard-working poor for productive activities. ITDP bicycles have multiplied the effectiveness of literacy teachers in Haiti, well drillers in Bolivia, and health workers in Nicaragua and Mozambique. A technical assistance project in Nicaragua trains local mechanics and has helped nongovernmental groups set up local assembly and repair shops. The institute is breaking further ground by promoting all-terrain bicycles—also called mountain bikes—more appropriate for rugged conditions than the half-century-old English roadster model usually found in the Third World.[69]

Experience in Asia has shown that starting a bicycle industry is a relatively low-risk venture for developing countries that have little industrial base. A small assembly plant and repair shop can run on about $200 worth of tools, and 100 bicycles can be manufactured for the energy and materials it takes to build a medium-sized car.[70]

India has demonstrated how a nearly self-sufficient bicycle industry can be created by first assembling bicycles with imported parts, then producing frames in local workshops, and gradually establishing small factories to produce parts domestically. From a modest beginning five decades ago, India has become a major world producer. It directs more than 90 percent of its bicycle exports to other developing countries, and through joint-venture and license agreements is sharing its small-scale, labor-intensive techniques with countries throughout Asia, Africa, and the Caribbean.[71]

> "Use of human powered vehicles is increasingly common among employees of development agencies, who find they are sometimes the only way to reach remote villages."

That there are only slightly more developing countries making bicy- **31** cles than producing automobiles—even though domestic auto man- ufacturing demands much more in capital, technical, and managerial resources—epitomizes the Third World's missed oppor- tunities with human powered vehicles. Engineer and urban planner Ricardo Navarro, who is nurturing a string of small workshops in El Salvador that he hopes will become a vigorous domestic bicycle industry, has succinctly described the potential role of pedal power. In Navarro's words, the bicycle is "a *mecanismo indispensable* for development."[72]

Cycling Societies

What sets apart the handful of countries that, in a world seduced by automobiles, have chosen to embrace the bicycle? These few cycling societies are not notably different, in terms of living standards, geog- raphy or climate, from their noncycling neighbors. (See Table 8.) A study by John Pucher of transport systems in 12 North American and Western European countries confirms that wide variations in people's transport decisions are not chiefly influenced by levels of income, technology, or urbanization. The difference lies in enlight- ened public policy and strong government support.[73]

Chinese authorities recognized decades ago that human powered transport could move more people more cheaply than any other option. They began investing in low-cost, mass production of bi- cycles when most people were still too poor to own one, and directed infrastructure improvements to nonmotorized travel. When com- mercial access to villages was opened in the early sixties, it was largely over rural tracks built for people moving on foot, animal carts, or bicycles.[74]

Special bicycle avenues with five to six lanes each are common in Chinese cities. Motorized traffic is often separated from pedestrians

Table 8. Cycling as Share of Daily Passenger Trips, Selected Cities

City	Percent of Daily Trips
Tianjin, China	77[1]
Shenyang, China	65
Groningen, Netherlands	50
Beijing, China	48
Delft, Netherlands	43
Dhaka, Bangladesh	40[2]
Erlangen, West Germany	26
Odense, Denmark	25
Tokyo, Japan	25[3]
Moscow, Soviet Union	24[3]
Delhi, India	22
Copenhagen, Denmark	20
Basel, Switzerland	20
Hannover, West Germany	14
Manhattan, United States	8[4]
Perth, Australia	6
Toronto, Canada	3[4]
London, England	2
Sydney, Australia	1

[1] Share of non-walking trips.
[2] Trips by cycle rickshaw only.
[3] Share cycling or walking to work.
[4] Vehicle trips (versus passenger trips).

Source: Worldwatch Institute, based on various sources.

and cyclists on three-track roads, and some cities set apart space for **33** load-carrying bicycles. Convenient guarded bicycle parking is plentiful, as are services for maintenance and repair. In addition to Beijing's 173 registered repair shops, more than 1,000 independent sidewalk mechanics repair bikes along the capital's streets. Throughout China, city governments have long used bicycles to relieve pressure on overcrowded buses by paying commuters a monthly allowance for cycling to work. China has thus provided high quality transport to large numbers of people while postponing the need for heavy public transit investments.[75]

This policy did not, however, foresee the bicycle boom of the eighties. The Kingdom of Bicycles now suffers from traffic jams, with bicycles and rickshaws fighting motor vehicles for road space. Some Chinese planners propose that bicyclists, just as car commuters in the industrial countries, should be encouraged to use the expanded fleet of public buses for longer commutes. Yet China's buses are crowded enough as it is, and the country will need an estimated 200,000 more buses by the year 2000 just to keep up with projected growth in demand. Commuter data suggest that, if half the people who commuted by bicycle in Beijing, Tianjin, and Shanghai in 1985 had decided to take the bus instead, roughly 12,000 more buses would have been needed in these three cities alone.[76]

Chinese authorities are trying a number of other solutions to bicycle congestion. Among them are efforts to move workers nearer to their workplaces and develop local business centers. Working hours are also staggered to spread traffic volume over more of the day. Professor Li Jia Ying at the Northern Transportation University in Beijing suggests giving priority to buses in some intersections and marking safe detours for bicycle traffic. Li further proposes to separate bicycles from each other by designating sub-lanes for cyclists riding at different speeds.[77]

Japan is another cycling society in which bicycle trips for practical use far outnumber those for leisure or sport. Census figures for 1980 showed that 7.2 million commuters—approximately 15 percent of

34   the total—rode bicycles to work or to commuter rail stations. Bicycle ownership has climbed from an average of 1 per household in 1970 to 1.5 today. Though recreational cycling is quickly gaining enthusiasts, most bicyclists ride for everyday shopping and commuting to work or school.[78]

Many of Japan's rail passengers pedal daily to train and subway stations. Since the sixties, Japanese transport has been dominated by commuter railroads that link urban centers to the rapidly growing suburbs. As development fanned out farther from the rail lines, many commuters switched from slow feeder buses to bikes to reach suburban stations. By the mid seventies, "bicycle pollution"—a phrase coined for the hundreds or even thousands of bicycles crammed in front of some railway stations—spurred the government to promote bike parking as a way out of the chaos.[79]

National legislation passed in 1980 empowers local governments to require that railways and private businesses build ample bicycle parking. The central government provides funding to help pay for construction. Today there are more than 8,600 official and private bicycle parking sites, with total capacity for 2.4 million bicycles, roughly half provided free of charge by national or local jurisdictions. Bike parking is also common at Japanese apartment complexes and in recreational and shopping areas.[80]

Limited land space in urban Japan—where downtown real estate can cost over $7,000 per square foot—has inspired the building of bicycle parking towers. Dozens of transit stations have multi-story structures in which automated cranes park thousands of bicycles. Another way Japanese planners save space is through suburban rental systems. These facilities hire out hundreds of bicycles, many of which serve more than one commuter a day.[81]

Cycling is likely to become even more important in Japan as the country is forced to control its growth in automobile use. The government makes car owners pay a $2,000 registration fee every two years for the entire life of the vehicle. If cycling is to take up the load as people seek less-expensive transport, local authorities will need to join such measures with more attention to cycling facilities and revamping the country's extensive but poor-quality cycle paths.[82]

The Netherlands and Denmark are Europe's exemplary cycling societies. "Bicycle tourism" is a major industry, with thousands of people taking extended trips along country roads to enjoy diverse landscapes and visit picturesque towns. Like elsewhere on the continent, pro-bicycle planning for utilitarian purposes in these countries is part of a recent search for alternatives to automobile dependence. But the bicycle's top two champions owe their current lead in cycling policy to having had a head start.[83]

The Netherlands has a long tradition of cycling both for recreation and everyday transportation. The bicycle's role declined, as in other industrial countries, in the fifties and sixties as more people bought automobiles. But cycling resurged when the repercussions of growing car use were dramatized by energy shocks and ecological crises in the seventies.[84]

Dutch officials realized that fostering cycling would not only improve the urban environment but also enhance the transport sector without having to pave over historic town centers or spend large amounts of public money. Between 1975 and 1985 the national government spent some $230 million to construct cycleways and parking, and increase transit access through bicycle facilities at rail stations. Highway construction expenditures, by contrast, began to decline; by the early eighties, funding for bicycle projects exceeded 10 percent of capital spending on roadways.[85]

In 1986 the Netherlands' cycle paths covered 13,500 kilometers. Perhaps even more significant than this achievement, however, are Dutch efforts to create direct, uninterrupted cycling routes—thus making riding practical, rather than simply getting cyclists out of the way of other traffic. As a result, the share of trips made by bicycle in Dutch towns and cities is typically between 20 and 50 percent.[86]

Groningen, the largest city in the northern Netherlands, has found an integrated approach more effective than providing isolated cycling facilities. Bicycle parking and cycling routes combined with well-planned traffic measures have raised the share of bicycling to half of all trips in the city. The city of Delft's cycling provisions include underpasses and bridges across dangerous intersections, and innovations in traffic management. For example, some traffic-activated signals, normally sensitive only to motor vehicles, detect bicycles as they arrive at intersections. Pavement lines at intersections allow cyclists space to stop ahead of other traffic and move first. Cyclists are also permitted to ride against the traffic on some one-way streets.[87]

Rather than replace the automobile, the Netherlands has sought to balance auto transport with bicycling, public transit, and walking as a national policy goal. Pedestrian-only streets and reduced speed limits are common in Dutch towns, and car parking is prohibited in many city streets. Residential streets are often transformed into *woonerven*, or "living yards," a traffic-calming concept introduced in the seventies. In a *woonerf* the road becomes a paved courtyard. All means of transport are allowed, but bicyclists and pedestrians have priority and cars enter only as "guests."[88]

A current car boom, however, is challenging Dutch officials to put their energies into simply maintaining the present popularity of cycling. In 1988, Dutch Transport Minister Nellie Smit-Kroes announced a bold plan not only to head off the expected growth in automobile numbers from the current 5 million to an estimated 8 million in 20 years, but to encourage a decline to just 3.5 million cars. Taxes will increase the costs of buying and driving a car by about half, while public transit will receive an extra $5.7 billion per year. A new electronic system will log the number of kilometers each car travels, and "excessive drivers" will then pay additional taxes.[89]

The Netherlands' closest peer in cycling is Denmark, where, as Copenhagen's Mayor of Traffic notes, poets have celebrated the bicycle and sculptors have made statues of cyclists. The share of bi-

"The Netherlands has sought to balance
auto transport with bicycling, public
transit, and walking as a national goal."

cycles in Denmark's traffic counts, though slightly lower than that in **37**
the Netherlands, is equally impressive; 20 percent of personal trips
in Danish cities and towns are made by bicycle. Danish rail stations
typically accommodate several hundred bikes at a time. A 1983 survey revealed that 32 percent of people traveled to work by bicycle,
and an additional 9 percent commuted by pedaling to the train.[90]

Since 1982 the national budget has allocated $7 to 13 million each
year for building commuter cycle lanes along major roads. Today
some 75 percent of major roads in Denmark have cycle tracks. Much
of the cycle network is the result of the Danish Cyclist Federation's
efforts, since its founding in 1905, to pressure authorities to accommodate cyclists with special facilities and traffic management.[91]

Use of cycle paths in Denmark and the Netherlands has traditionally
been mandatory where they parallel major high-speed roads, caus-
ing some controversy among riders. Experience has shown, however, that if they are of high quality, cyclists will readily use them
whether mandatory or not.[92]

Denmark has also sought to tame the automobile through taxation of
car ownership and use. Gasoline prices are among the highest in
Europe, and the Danish Ministry of Transport describes the 186-per-
cent sales tax on new cars—compared with 47 percent in the
Netherlands and 5 percent in the United States—as paying for three
cars and getting only one.[93]

North America's closest approach to a cycling society is the bicycle-
friendly university town. Two such communities in northern
California, Palo Alto and Davis, vie for the title of bicycling capital of
the United States. Davis has the higher cycling rate of the two—25
percent of total trips in the community of 44,000 are made by
bike—and cycle trailers filled with groceries or children are not an
unusual sight. Davis has some 30 miles of bicycle lanes for 100 miles
of streets, and roughly 20 miles of separate cycle paths.[94]

Palo Alto, an affluent, highly educated community of 56,000 near

38 San Francisco, has gone beyond physical improvements to promote bicycle transportation. The city government pays its employees seven cents a mile for all business travel by bicycle, and sponsors a city-wide monthly "Leave Your Car at Home Day." Palo Alto's police department has a bicycle squad. The city has a traffic school for juveniles who violate bicycle laws and funds an on-road cycling course for middle school students.[95]

Palo Alto has spent roughly $1 million since 1980—mostly from state grants—on bicycle lockers and racks, bike bridges, and lighted cycle paths. All road patching in town must adhere to high smoothness standards. Bicycle-detecting traffic sensors are clearly marked so that cyclists can easily activate them. The centerpiece of Palo Alto's 40-mile system of bikeways is its bicycle boulevard, a two-mile stretch in the middle of town where bikes are the only through traffic allowed. The bicycle boulevard is just the first segment of a larger network planned for the city center.[96]

A 1983 zoning ordinance requires new buildings beyond a certain size to provide secure bicycle parking and showers for employees. Several large employers in Palo Alto add their own incentives. The Alza Corporation, for example, pays bicycle commuters $1 for each day they ride to work. Amenities at Xerox—which include a towel service in the shower room—help explain why 20 percent of the company's local employees cycle to work, one of the highest bicycle commuter rates nationwide.[97]

In many parts of the United States, public support for cycling facilities has suffered from a deep divide among cycling advocates. On one side are those who oppose any special cycleways or routes that are separate from motor vehicle traffic, believing them unsafe and discriminatory. On the other side are cyclists who advocate building special bikeways where practical.

This division has undermined official cycling promotion, since many local authorities dismiss requests for new bikeways on the grounds that cyclists themselves do not want them. Meanwhile, millions of people annually use the 2,700 miles of abandoned rail corridors that have been converted into cycling and hiking trails largely through the efforts of the Rails-To-Trails Conservancy—a private organization.[98]

Scattered but thriving bicycle programs outside the main cycling societies show a growing trend toward pro-bicycle planning. Many towns in Sweden, Switzerland, and West Germany have steadily increasing shares of cyclists in their traffic, and national and local authorities have stepped up their commitment to cycle planning in recent years. West Germany's years of *Verkehrsberuhigung*, or traffic calming, have helped foster a cycling environment by restraining motorized traffic with physical barriers and reduced speed limits. Swedish towns have experimented with restraining motor vehicles since the seventies by using "traffic cells" that divide a city into zones to reroute traffic from denser areas onto main roads, making smaller streets safer for cycling and walking.[99]

Several cities in Canada and Australia are drafting or implementing cycling plans. Montreal—a city with four to five months of hard winter—plans to double its present 200 kilometers of bikeways by the year 1993, aiming to have a cycle lane or path within 2 kilometers of every point on the city's street system. Melbourne, Perth, and other Australian cities are following the example of the city of Geelong's 1977 bicycle plan, which aims to make every street bikable.[100]

There is ample proof that a cycling society can emerge out of one already hooked on the automobile. Palo Alto Council member Ellen Fletcher, who cycles to city meetings and has become known nationally for her bicycle advocacy, knows how to fulfill the bicycle's potential. "All you have to do is make it easier to ride a bike than drive a car," she says. "People will take it from there."[101]

Getting There From Here

In a 1988 *Newsweek* interview on the U.S. gridlock predicament, former FHWA traffic systems chief Lyle Saxton remarked: "We have

Table 9. Taxes on Auto Ownership and Gasoline Compared with
Kilometers of Auto Travel, Selected Countries

	Gasoline Sales Tax[1]	Automobile Sales Tax[2]	Kilometers Driven per Person
	(percent)	(percent)	(thousand per year)
Denmark	355	186	4.2
Italy	285	22	3.4
Netherlands	245	47	3.9
Belgium	178	25	4.2
Great Britain	178	25	4.3
Switzerland	170	8	6.0
Austria	150	52	3.4
West Germany	138	14	4.6
Sweden	133	41	8.0
United States	45	5	7.7

[1] 1987 data.
[2] 1982 data.

Source: Adapted from John Pucher, "Urban Travel Behavior as the Outcome of Public Policy: The Example of Modal-split in Western Europe," *APA Journal*, Autumn, 1988.

built our society around the automobile and we have to deal with it." But as the world's cycling societies demonstrate, neither governments nor citizens need accept the status quo. With public policy support and private initiatives on many levels—from international institutions to the individual commuter—bicycle transportation can become an everyday alternative.[102]

National governments can make automobile owners pay more of the hidden expenses of driving. The costs of these items—including road building and maintenance, police and fire services, accidents

"In the United States, the hidden
cost of car driving may
total $300 billion each year."

and health care—are borne by all taxpayers, drivers and non-drivers   **41**
alike. In the United States the hidden price of car driving may total
as much as $300 billion each year.[103]

One way to counteract this enormous subsidy is for governments to
tax auto ownership and use, and invest the revenues in mass transit
and in cycling and pedestrian facilities. In John Pucher's recent
study of 12 countries in Western Europe and North America, it is
clear that when drivers are made to pay the costs of automobile travel through taxation of ownership and use, total mileage driven tends
to decline. (See Table 9.)[104]

Of the countries in the study, Denmark and the Netherlands—the
two with among the highest taxes—also have among the lowest figures for per capita kilometers of automobile travel. The United
States comes in last in both sales and gasoline taxation, and is second
only to Sweden—the country with the next-to-lowest gasoline tax
—in kilometers of auto travel per person. Moreover, while the
United States puts these tax monies into highway expenditures, the
European countries put most of the proceeds into general revenues.[105]

According to Pucher's analysis, Americans do not drive more
because of greater affluence; 7 of the 10 European countries in the
study had higher per capita incomes than the United States in 1980.
Greater distances account for some of the difference, as well as variations in urban land use. Perhaps most important is the relative
scarcity of mass transit service—as little as a quarter of that in other
countries in the sample, measured on a per capita basis.[106]

Taxes can also encourage the private sector to charge user fees for
such valuable resources as parking space. In the United States, 75
percent of all commuters have free parking provided by employers,
a tax-free fringe benefit for employees and a tax-deductible expense
for businesses that provide it. In Japan and much of Europe, in contrast, public policy makes parking both more expensive and less
available.[107]

42 The principle of a user fee can be extended to another amenity—road space. While many countries use highway tolls to help defray the costs of road building and maintenance, Singapore charges private cars carrying fewer than four passengers "congestion fees" for entering the downtown area during rush hours. Since 1975 the scheme has raised Singapore's average downtown traffic speeds by 20 percent and reduced traffic accidents by 25 percent. Savings in fuel consumption are estimated at 30 percent.[108]

As the world's cities rapidly grow larger, expanding mass transit systems will become increasingly important. Third World governments straining to extend public transit service to outlying settlements can maximize access to these systems by facilitating bike-and-ride.

Bike-and-ride facilities in the industrial world are an alternative to increased car commuting both between city centers and suburbs and from one suburb to another. Transit authorities have typically tried to attract passengers by building automobile parking lots, which require at least 20 times as much space as bicycle parking. For a small fraction of the cost of auto parking lots, secure bicycle facilities can increase convenient access to transit stations by a radius of at least 1 to 3 kilometers, enlarging the total practical area served roughly ninefold. Bicycle lockers and garages can serve commuters for whom either the home or workplace—but not both—is within walking distance of a station. The commuter can then cycle between the station and whichever destination is farther, storing the bicycle securely all day or overnight. Permits that allow bicycles on trains and buses make it unnecessary for either transit stop to be near the commuter's destination.[109]

Leaders in the developing world can make national transportation policies more effective by considering the mobility and access needs of their impoverished majorities. Where affordability is a major issue, providing people credit for purchasing bicycles and other low-cost vehicles is crucial. Particularly in countries that discriminate against rickshaw drivers and others, a first step is to correct bias

against human power and focus on improving rickshaws, not banning them. Governments may need to balance motorized transit
investments with less costly bicycle subsidies and cycling infrastructure.

Governments can also foster domestic bicycle industries, while
avoiding heavy import taxes and other policies that have overpro-
tected them and, eventually, led to factory closings in countries like
Kenya and Tanzania. It is important for authorities to encourage the
flow of technologies from elsewhere in the developing world, and
support research in adapting low-cost vehicles to local conditions.[110]

Multilateral banks and other development organizations can help
spur these changes. The World Bank, for example, emphasizes bicycles and low-cost roads in several projects that are part of the Sub-
Saharan Africa Transport Program, an ongoing, joint undertaking
with the United Nations Development Program, the United Nations
Economic Commission for Africa, and several bilateral donors that
in 1987 began to reevaluate the ineffective, motor-biased transport
policies of the region.[111]

The bank's series of nonmotorized transport projects seeks to
address the problems of rural access, focusing on trips that take
place off the road network and on the transport needs of women.
Studies from experience in Africa and elsewhere—including Brazil,
Colombia, India, and Nepal—will be used to help formulate new
recommendations aimed at policymakers and local transport officials.[112]

Local governments in developing and industrial countries alike can
promote cycling more effectively by creating an official bicycle advisory council that reports to the mayor, city council, or equivalent
authority. This advisory body can help decision makers ensure that
all transport improvements consider the needs of cyclists. Building
codes and ordinances can specify that new developments beyond a
given size must include bicycle parking and showers for commuters,
and that new or rebuilt roads and bridges include safe bicycle access.

44 A specific portion of downtown parking space can be devoted to bicycles and a percentage of all transport spending allocated to cycling facilities.[113]

No single type of cycleway is appropriate for every place or for every rider. Which kind of facility serves best—whether a bicycle lane, bike path, or route markings on regular roads—depends on both the setting and the cyclist. Differences in moving speeds, volume of traffic, and skill levels all should be taken into account.

It is important that cycleways separating bicycles from motorized traffic be well-designed and maintained; otherwise, they give inferior access compared with motorable roads, and can be more dangerous. Traffic authorities can improve cyclists' safety on regular streets at little cost by removing debris and modifying wheel-trapping drain grates.

Traffic management is important in balancing the needs of all types of vehicles, particularly where limited space makes physical separation impossible. For decades the Netherlands has led the way in calming traffic with *woonerven*, and West Germany with *Verkehrsberuhigung* and reduced speed limits. These moves can create a system in which urban form and traffic restraint help all means of transportation to safely coexist.

Despite progress in recent years with better traffic management and road designs, cyclists are still more vulnerable than drivers. Safety education for all road users and law enforcement for offenders are crucial—for riders and drivers alike. In Manhattan, a decline in bicycle-pedestrian accidents each year since 1985 is credited in part to increased police vigilance in issuing summonses to cyclists, and in part to the emphasis by cycling organizations on mutual responsibility and cooperation.[114]

The long-term interests of cities will be best served if metropolitan areas of 50,000 people or more adopt regional planning and create growth plans that limit urban sprawl. Innovative land use plans

> "Each time a driver makes a trip
> by cycle instead of by automobile,
> not only the cyclist but society
> as a whole reaps the benefits."

cluster homes, shopping, and workplaces and base layouts as much **45**
as possible on cycling and walking distances, with emphasis on public transit to complete the transport balance.[115]

Government action—from national taxation policies to local provi-
sion of bicycle racks—is not likely to happen without a concerted
effort from cycling advocacy groups and individuals acting to
counter the strong automobile lobbies. Local bike clubs with a handful of members and international groups with tens of thousands may
be the most powerful forces for this broadening of transport alternatives. When Mayor Edward Koch announced in 1987 that New York
City's three main avenues would be closed to bicycles on weekdays,
cycling advocacy groups demonstrated against the ban, took legal
action to reverse it on a technical flaw, and finally persuaded the
mayor not to try banning bicycles again.[116]

In June 1989, the League of American Wheelmen, a national cycling
organization founded in 1880, held the first National Congress of
Bicyclists since cycling's Golden Age in the 1890s. The congress
established several goals, from urging local officials to enforce traffic
laws that affect cyclists, to persuading the U.S. Department of
Transportation to include cycling in national transportation policy.[117]

Perhaps the greatest potential for change lies with the individual
cyclist. Pressing employers and local authorities to provide cycling
facilities—and simply using bicycles whenever possible—can have a
great impact. Some cyclists can make all the difference in simply
leading by example; Argentine President Carlos Menem has urged
citizens to ease the shock of soaring gasoline prices by riding bicycles—and is a cyclist himself.[118]

Each time a driver makes a trip by bicycle instead of by automobile,
not only the cyclist but society as a whole reaps the benefits. One of
the greatest ironies of the twentieth century is that around the globe,
vast amounts of such priceless things as land, petroleum, and clean
air have been relinquished for motorization—and yet most people in
the world will never own an automobile. As author and cyclist

46 James McGurn writes, "The bicycle is the vehicle of a new mentality. It quietly challenges a system of values which condones dependency, wastage, inequality of mobility, and daily carnage. . . . There is every reason why cycling should be helped to enjoy another Golden Age."[119]

Notes

1. Number of bicycles worldwide is author's estimate based on **47** sources cited in Tables 1 and 2; number of automobiles (394 million in 1987) is from Motor Vehicle Manufacturers Association (MVMA), *Facts and Figures '89* (Detroit, Mich.: 1989).

2. James McGurn, *On Your Bicycle: An Illustrated History of Cycling* (London: John Murray Publishers, Ltd., 1987).

3. Michael A. Replogle, "Let them Drive Cars," *The New Internationalist*, May 1989.

4. Michael A. Replogle, *Bicycles and Public Transportation: New Links to Suburban Transit Markets*, 2nd ed. (Washington, D.C.: The Bicycle Federation, 1988).

5. R.H. ter Heide, "Recreational Use of the Bicycle, Organizational and Economic Aspects," *Velo City 87 International Congress: Planning for the Urban Cyclist*, proceedings of the Third International Velo City Congress, Groningen, the Netherlands, September 22–26, 1987 (hereinafter cited as Velo City 87 Conference); In 1986 the Netherlands had some 120 passenger cars per square kilometer. Only Hong Kong and Singapore had more, with 175 and 400 cars per square kilometer, respectively; MVMA, *Facts and Figures '88* (Detroit, Mich.: 1988).

6. "Population Control Comes in the 'Kingdom of Bikes,'" *China Daily*, January 9, 1989; Jun-Men Yang, "Bicycle Traffic in China," *Transportation Quarterly*, January 1985.

7. "See the PRC in Your Xiali," *Asiaweek*, September 2, 1988; Jun-Men Yang, "Bicycle Traffic in China."

8. Zhou You Ma, "Ode to the Bicycle," *China Reconstructs*, 1987; Jun-Men Yang, "Bicycle Traffic in China"; *Japan Cycle Press International*, October 1988.

9. V. Setty Pendakur, "Formal and Informal Urban Transport in Asia," *CUSO Journal*, December 1987; for a full description of differ-

48 ent kinds of paratransit, see Peter J. Rimmer, *Rikisha to Rapid Transit: Urban Public Transport Systems and Policy in Southeast Asia* (Sydney: Pergamon Press, 1986); Ken Hughes and Michael A. Replogle, "Sustainable Transportation," *Not Man Apart*, July/August 1987.

10. David Mozer, director, International Bicycle Fund, private communication, August 4, 1989.

11. Mozer, private communication, August 4, 1989; Ken Hughes, executive director, Institute for Transportation and Development Policy (ITDP), private communication, August 9, 1989.

12. Richard Barret, World Bank, private communication, March 24, 1989; Mozer, private communication, August 4, 1989.

13. Ricardo A. Navarro, Urs Heierli, and Victor Beck, *Alternativas de Transporte en América Latina: La Bicicleta y los Triciclos*, Swiss Center for Appropriate Technology (St. Gallen: 1985); Ken Hughes, private communication, April 7, 1989.

14. Werner Brög et al., "Promotion and Planning for Bicycle Transportation: An International Overview," paper presented at annual meeting of the Transportation Research Board, Washington, D.C., January 1984.

15. Number of bicycles per person based on sources cited in Table 1; Andy Clarke, "Pro-bike: A Cycling Policy for the 1990s" (Friends of the Earth: London, 1987); the Bicycle Institute of America, Inc., estimates that in 1988 there were 2.7 million bicycle commuters in the United States.

16. Figures for ownership based on sources cited in Table 2.

17. See, for example, in John Pucher, "Urban Travel Behavior as the Outcome of Public Policy: The Example of Modal-split in Western Europe and North America," *APA Journal*, Autumn 1988: "A few regions of the United States are as flat and as densely populated as

the Netherlands and thus potentially as conducive to bicycling. Yet **49** nowhere in the United States does bicycling even approach the level of importance it holds for the Dutch. The northern European countries especially provide extensive, coordinated networks of bikeways in both urban and rural areas, and they either give bicycle traffic priority over autos or at least treat it equally"; Replogle, *Bicycles and Public Transportation;* Andy Clarke, government relations director, League of American Wheelmen, private communication, March 16, 1989; Clarke, "Pro-bike: A Cycling Policy for the 1990s."

18. Alethea Morison, Bicycle Institute of New South Wales, private communication, June 1, 1989; James C. McCullagh, "10 Best Cycling Cities," *Bicycling,* November 1988.

19. *Human Power*, Technical Journal of the International Human Powered Vehicle Association, Inc., various editions.

20. Production figures based on sources cited in Table 3; "NICs Update," *Japan Cycle Press International*, June 1988.

21. For a thorough discussion of traffic accidents and other consequences of excessive reliance on cars, see Michael Renner, *Rethinking the Role of the Automobile*, Worldwatch Paper 84 (Washington, D.C.: Worldwatch Institute, June 1988).

22. Michael P. Walsh, "The Global Importance of Motor Vehicles in the Climate Modification Problem," *International Environment Reporter*, May 1989; Richard Gould, "The Exhausting Options of Modern Vehicles," *New Scientist*, May 13, 1989; Renner, *Rethinking the Role of the Automobile.*

23. Global Environment Monitoring System, *Assessment of Urban Air Quality* (Nairobi, Kenya: United Nations Environment Program and World Health Organization, 1988).

24. Melinda Warren and Kenneth Chilton, "Clearing the Air of Ozone," *Society*, March/April 1989; Don R. Clay, hearing before the

50 Subcommittee on Health and the Environment of the Committee on Energy and Commerce, U.S. House of Representatives, February 28, 1989; "New Mexican President Promises Action to Control Air Pollution," *Multinational Environmental Outlook*, December 22, 1988; "Air Pollution in Brazil," *Multinational Environmental Outlook*, July 21, 1988.

25. Renner, *Rethinking the Role of the Automobile*.

26. James J. MacKenzie, *Breathing Easier: Taking Action on Climate Change, Air Pollution, and Energy Insecurity* (Washington, D.C.: World Resources Institute, 1988); James J. Mackenzie and Mohamed T. El-Ashry, "Ill Winds: Air Pollution's Toll on Trees and Crops," *Technology Review*, April 1989.

27. Renner, *Rethinking the Role of the Automobile*; Gould, "The Exhausting Options of Modern Vehicles"; Walsh, "The Global Importance of Motor Vehicles in the Climate Modification Problem."

28. U.S. Department of Energy, Energy Information Administration, *Monthly Energy Review*, March 1989; Jeffry J. Erickson, David L. Greene, and Alberto J. Sabadell, "An Analysis of Transportation Energy Conservation Projects in Developing Countries," *Transportation*, Vol. 1, No. 5, 1988.

29. Deborah Bleviss, *The New Oil Crisis and Fuel Economy Technologies: Preparing the Light Transportation Industry for the 1990's* (New York: Quorum Press, 1988).

30. "Traffic Jams: The City, the Commuter and the Car," *The Economist*, February 18, 1989.

31. Melinda Beck, "Smart Cars, Smart Streets," *Newsweek*, December 5, 1988; "Taibei Residents Troubled by Traffic Tangle," *China Daily*, August 30, 1988; "Commuters' Nine to Five Favourites," *South*, November 1988; O'seun Ogunseitan, "Wednesday Is an Odd Day in Lagos," *New Internationalist*, May 1989.

32. "Traffic Jams 'Cost Britain 15 Billion Pounds a Year,'" *The London Times*, March 30, 1989; "Traffic Jams," *The Economist*; Robert D. Ervin and Kan Chen, "Toward Motoring Smart," *Issues in Science and Technology*, Winter 1988–89.

33. James J. MacKenzie, *Breathing Easier*; Andy Clarke, "How to Use Bicycling as a Cost-effective Means of Reducing Air Pollution," League of American Wheelmen, Baltimore, Maryland, 1989.

34. John Young, "Methanol Moonshine," *World Watch*, July/August 1988.

35. Jillian Beardwood and John Elliott, "Roads Generate Traffic," paper prepared for the Greater London Council, 1985; Mick Hamer, "Splitting the City," *New Internationalist*, May 1989.

36. See, for example, Renner, *Rethinking the Role of the Automobile*; Robert D. Ervin and Kan Chen, "Toward Motoring Smart," *Issues in Science and Technology*, Winter 1988–89.

37. Renner, *Rethinking the Role of the Automobile*; China's sown area in 1986 was approximately 144 million hectares; *China Agricultural Yearbook 1987* (Beijing: Agricultural Publishing House, 1987).

38. Clarke, "How to Use Bicycling as a Cost-effective Means of Reducing Air Pollution"; MVMA, *Facts and Figures '88*; Clarke, "Pro-bike: A Cycling Policy for the 1990s"; unfortunately, dangerously high pollution levels are even more of a health threat to people who are exercising outdoors, including cyclists. Air pollution during such periods becomes, ironically, a deterrent to bicycling. Until air quality improves, cyclists need a workable alternative—ideally, mass transit—on particularly hazy days. Eventually, when more drivers have switched to bicycling the air will likely be safer for everyone.

39. Replogle, *Bicycles and Public Transportation*.

40. Andy Clarke, "Air Pollution: What's In It For Bicyclists?" *Bicycle*

52 *USA*, December 1988; Ross Ruske, bicycle coordinator, U.S. Environmental Protection Agency, private communication, July 6, 1989.

41. Edward Cody, "Dutch Outline Proposal to Protect Environment," *Washington Post*, May 26, 1989; Clarke, "Air Pollution: What's in It For Bicyclists?"

42. Mary C. Holcomb et al., *Transportation Energy Data Book: Edition 9* (Oak Ridge, Tenn.: Oak Ridge National Laboratory, 1987).

43. Clarke, "Pro-Bike: A Cycling Policy for the 1990s."

44. Replogle, *Bicycles and Public Transportation;* Alan E. Pisarski, *Commuting in America: A National Report on Commuting Patterns and Trends* (Westport, Conn.: Eno Foundation for Transportation, 1987).

45. United Nations, *Transportation Strategies for Human Settlements in Developing Countries* (Nairobi: Center for Human Settlements (Habitat), 1984).

46. "Biking Sundays Return Bogotá to Citizens," *Edmonton Journal*, October 30, 1987.

47. Ivan Illich, *Toward a History of Needs* (Berkeley: Heydey Books, 1977).

48. Study done by psychologist Raymond Novaco at the University of California at Irvine cited in "Gridlock! Congestion on America's Highways and Runways Takes a Grinding Toll," *Time*, September 12, 1988; physical benefits of cycling from Nelson Pena, "Survival of the Fittest," *Bicycling*, June 1988.

49. Charles Komanoff is president of Transportation Alternatives, a cycling advocacy group in New York City; quote from Komanoff, "The Bike Ban is Bad Medicine," *The New York Observer*, January 25, 1988.

50. Automobile prices based on 1983 market price for an economy car in some 25 developing countries, from the World Bank, *Urban Transport: A World Bank Policy Study* (Washington, D.C.: 1986); bicycle prices assumed to range from $80 to $250.

51. V. Setty Penkakur, *Urban Growth, Urban Poor and Urban Transport in Asia* (Vancouver: University of British Columbia, 1986).

52. World Bank, *Urban Transport: A World Bank Policy Study*, and other World Bank documents.

53. On public versus private bus services, see Alan Armstrong-Wright and Sebastien Thiriez, *Bus Services: Reducing Costs, Raising Standards*, World Bank Technical Paper Number 68 (Washington, D.C.: World Bank, 1987); Delhi survey, V. Setty Pendakur, "Urban Transport Planning and the Urban Poor," *Journal of the Indian Roads Congress*, September 1984; in Indian cities, a new bicycle costs less than a year's worth of bus fares for the journey to work; A.G. Hathway, "Travel Requirements of the Urban Poor," unpublished paper, Bristol Polytechnic, United Kingdom, 1989.

54. Val Curtis, *Women and the Transport of Water* (London: Intermediate Technology Publications, 1986); Charles K. Kaira, *Transportation Needs of the Rural Population in Developing Countries: An Approach to Improved Transportation Planning*, doctoral dissertation, University of Karlsruhe, West Germany, 1983; I. Barwell, G.A. Edmonds, J.D.G.F. Howe, and J. de Veen, *Rural Transport in Developing Countries* (London: Intermediate Technology Publications, 1985).

55. Paul Zille, "Transport Research: An Investigation into Local Level Transport Characteristics and Requirements in Ismani Division, Iringa, Tanzania," Project Report, Intermediate Technology Transport, Ltd., Oxon, United Kingdom, 1988; Gordon Hathway, *Low-cost Vehicles: Options for Moving People and Goods* (London: Intermediate Technology Publications, 1985); United Nations, *Transportation Strategies for Human Settlements in Developing Countries*.

54   **56.** Thampil Pankaj, World Bank, private communication, February 22, 1989.

57. Thampil Pankaj, World Bank, private communication, February 22, 1989; for men's participation in these chores, see Val Curtis, *Women and the Transport of Water*.

58. Hathway, *Low-cost Vehicles*; "Bicycle Adapted for New Uses for Indian Farmers," *The New York Times*, October 16, 1980; Job S. Ebenezer, associate director, World Hunger Program of the Evangelical Lutheran Church in America, private communication, August 1, 1989; "Rescue the Rickshaw," *New Internationalist*, May 1989.

59. S.V. Sethuraman, ed., *The Urban Informal Sector in Developing Countries: Employment, Poverty and Environment* (Geneva: International Labor Organization, 1981); "Bike—an Indispensable Tool," *China Daily*, February 1989; V. Setty Pendakur, "Formal and Informal Urban Transport in Asia," *CUSO Journal*, December 1987; Robin Stallings, "The Present Role of the Bicycle in Iran, Afghanistan, Pakistan, and India," ITDP, Washington, D.C., 1981.

60. Steven R. Weisman, "For the Poor of Calcutta, a Threat to Mobility," *New York Times*, February 10, 1988; Guy Dimond, "Wheels of Change in Bangladesh," *New Cyclist*, Winter 1988; Rebecca L. Reichmann and Ron Weber, "Solidarity in Development: The *Tricicleros* of Santo Domingo," *Grassroots Development*, Vol. 11, No. 2, 1987.

61. Pendakur, *Urban Growth, Urban Poor and Urban Transport in Asia*; Pendakur, "Formal and Informal Urban Transport in Asia."

62. S. Carapetis, H.L. Beenhakker, and J.D.F. Howe, *The Supply and Quality of Rural Transport Services in Developing Countries: A Comparative Review* (Washington, D.C.: World Bank, 1984); Studies on small-farmer transport needs include Kaira, *Transportation Needs of the Rural Population in Developing Countries: An Approach to*

Improved Transportation Planning; Barwell, Edmonds, Howe, and de Veen, *Rural Transport in Developing Countries*; Ian Barwell, John Howe, and Paul Zille, *Household Time Use and Agricultural Productivity in Sub-Saharan Africa: A Synthesis of I.T. Transport Research* (Oxon, United Kingdom: I.T. Transport, Ltd., 1987); Zille, "Transport Research: An Investigation into Local Level Transport Characteristics and Requirements in Ismani Division"; Hathway, *Low-cost Vehicles*; United Nations, *Transportation Strategies for Human Settlements in Developing Countries.*; quote from Wilfred Owen, *Transportation and World Development* (Baltimore: Johns Hopkins University Press, 1987).

63. Michael A. Replogle, "Transportation Strategies for Sustainable Development," paper prepared for Fifth World Conference on Transport Research, Yokohama, Japan, July 1989; *Washington Post*, April 23, 1987; Guy Dimond, "Wheels of Change in Bangladesh"; Alain Boebion, "Indonesia Sinks Symbol of Free Enterprise," *The Australian*, April 26, 1989; U.N. Department of International Economic and Social Affairs, *Population Growth and Policies in Mega-Cities: Dhaka* (New York: United Nations, 1987); Sethuraman, ed., *The Urban Informal Sector in Developing Countries: Employment, Poverty and Environment.*

64. Replogle, "Transportation Strategies for Sustainable Development"; Pendakur, "Formal and Informal Urban Transport in Asia."

65. Michael A. Replogle, "Sustainable Transportation Strategies for Third World Development," paper presented at the Transportation Research Board Annual Meeting, Washington, D.C., January 1988; World Bank document cited is "China Transport Sector Study," World Bank, Washington, D.C., 1985.

66. Original support for the Association of Tricicleros came from the Fundación para el Desarrollo Dominicano (FDD), a local private development agency that became "the first private voluntary organization in the Dominican Republic to offer loans to the urban poor."

56 The association also received technical assistance from Massachusetts-based Acción Internacional and funding from the Inter-American Foundation; see Rebecca L. Reichmann and Ron Weber, "Solidarity in Development: The *Tricicleros* of Santo Domingo"; Stephen Vetter, "Building the Infrastructure for Progress: Private Development Organizations in the Dominican Republic," *Grassroots Development*, Vol. 10, No. 1, 1986.

67. Thampil Pankaj, World Bank, private communication, February 22, 1989; Marcia D. Lowe, "Ghana Takes the Low-cost Road," *World Watch*, May/June, 1989.

68. McGurn, *On Your Bicycle.*

69. Hughes, numerous private communications; Barbara Francisco, "The Third World: Making it Mobile," *Washington Post*, January 30, 1989; Keith Oberg, "Beira: Low-cost Vehicle Demonstration Project," paper prepared for ITDP Bikes for Africa Program, Washington, D.C., 1989; the several other groups active in research and technical support for bicycle promotion in developing countries include the Swiss Center for Appropriate Technology (SKAT), the Netherlands-based Center for International Cooperation and Appropriate Technology, and the German Appropriate Technology Center.

70. Asian producers include China, Taiwan, Japan, India, Indonesia, Malaysia, Korea, and Thailand; "Promotion of Bicycle and Tricycle Use in El Salvador," Centro Salvadoreño de Tecnología Apropiada, San Salvador, 1986; Navarro, Heierli, and Beck, *La Bicicleta y los Triciclos.*

71. Navarro, Heierli, and Beck, *La Bicicleta y los Triciclos*; International Trade Center UNCTAD/GATT, *Bicycles and Components: A Pilot Survey of Opportunities for Trade among Developing Countries* (Geneva: United Nations, 1985).

72. Navarro, Heierli, and Beck, *La Bicicleta y los Triciclos.*

73. Pucher, "Urban Travel Behavior."

74. Carapetis, Beenhakker, and Howe, *The Supply and Quality of Rural Transport Services in Developing Countries.*

75. Wang Dazi, "Touring Beijing on a Rented Bike," *China Daily*, January 25, 1989; Li Jia Ying, "Management of Bicycling in Urban Areas," *Transportation Quarterly*, October 1987; Michael A. Powills and Chen Sheng-Hong, "Bicycles in Shanghai: A Major Transportation Issue," paper presented at Transportation Research Board annual meeting, Washington, D.C., January 1989; Wang Zhi Hao, "Bicycles in Large Cities in China," *Transport Reviews*, Vol. 9, No. 2, 1989.

76. Huichun Zhao, "Bicycles in Tianjin, China: A Case Study," Center for Advanced Research in Transportation, Arizona State University, Tempe, August 1987; Wang Zhi Hao, "Bicycles in Large Cities in China," *Transport Reviews*, Vol. 9, No. 2. , 1989; Huichun Zhao, "Bicycles in Tianjin, China; Tai Ming Cheung, "Road Works Ahead: Traffic Congestion Is Choking China's Cities," *Far Eastern Economic Review*, July 7, 1988.

77. Tai Ming Cheung, "Road Works Ahead"; Li Jia Ying, "Management of Bicycling in Urban Areas," *Transportation Quarterly*, October 1987.

78. Ryozo Tsutsumi, "Bicycle Safety and Parking Systems in Japan," *Pro Bike 88*, proceedings of the 5th International Conference on Bicycle Programs and Promotions, Tucson, Arizona, October 8–12, 1988; Replogle, private communication, August 9, 1989; Tsutsumi, "Bicycle Safety and Parking Systems in Japan."

79. Replogle, *Bicycles and Public Transportation.*

80. Tsutsumi, "Bicycle Safety and Parking Systems in Japan."

81. Tsutsumi, "Bicycle Safety and Parking Systems in Japan";

58 Replogle, private communication, August 19, 1989; Replogle, *Bicycles and Public Transportation*.

82. Replogle, private communication, August 9, 1989; Tsutsumi, "Bicycle Safety and Parking Systems in Japan."

83. Ter Heide, "Recreational Use of the Bicycle, Organizational and Economic Aspects," Velo City '87 Conference.

84. McGurn, *On Your Bicycle*.

85. A. Wilmink, "The Effects of State Subsidizing of Bicycle Facilities," Velo City '87 Conference; Michael A. Replogle, "Major Bikeway Construction Effort in the Netherlands," *Urban Transportation Abroad*, Winter 1982.

86. Ter Heide, "Recreational Use of the Bicycle," Velo City '87 Conference; M.J.P.F. Gommers, "The Bicycle Network of Delft, Influence on Trip-level, Network Use and Route Choice of Cyclists," Velo City '87 Conference.

87. Clarke, private communication, March 16, 1989; Dutch Ministry of Transport and Public Works, "Evaluation of the Delft Bicycle Network: Final Summary Report," The Hague, Netherlands, 1987; Dirk H. ten Grotenhuis, "The Delft Cycle Plan: Characteristics of the Concept," Velo City '87 Conference.

88. Transportation Environmental Studies of London (TEST), *Quality Streets: How Traditional Urban Centres Benefit from Traffic-calming*, London, 1988.

89. Debora MacKenzie, "Dutch Lead Drive to Banish Car Pollution," *New Scientist*, December 24, 1988; "Dutch Courage," *New Cyclist*, Spring 1989.

90. Gunna Starck, in Niels Jensen and Jens Erik Larsen, *Cycling in Denmark: From the Past into the Future*, issued by the Road

Directorate, Ministry of Transport, and the Municipality of Copenhagen, Copenhagen, 1989; Pucher, "Urban Travel Behavior"; Replogle, *Bicycles and Public Transportation*; Clarke, "Pro-Bike: A Cycling Policy for the 1990s."

91. Thomas Krag, Dansk Cyklist Forbund, private communication, July 18, 1989; Jensen and Larsen, *Cycling in Denmark*.

92. Similar controversy arises in any situation in which a separate facility for bicycles is inferior to that for motor traffic. Accordingly, the better solution is to make special cycling facilities equal in quality to regular motorized ones.

93. Pucher, "Urban Travel Behavior."

94. David Peltz, Davis Department of Public Works, private communication, July 28, 1989.

95. Gail Likens, Palo Alto transportation planner, private communication, July 28, 1989; Ray Hosler, "Best Bike Town Listing Leaves Davis Spinning its Wheels," *San Francisco Chronicle*, December 12, 1988; Lisa Lapin, "CBS News Sees P.A. as the Bicycle Capital," *San Jose Mercury News*, August 23, 1988; Ellen Fletcher, Palo Alto City Council member, private communication, August 7, 1989.

96. Likens, private communication, July 28, 1989; Jane Gross, "Palo Alto Journal: Where Bicycle is King (And the Queen, Too)," *New York Times*, June 26, 1989; Lapin, "CBS News Sees P.A. as the Bicycle Capital"; Ellen Fletcher, private communication, August 7, 1989.

97. Lapin, "CBS News sees P.A. as the Bicycle Capital."

98. Rails-to-Trails Conservancy, "Restoring Life to Abandoned Railroad Corridors," Washington, D.C., 1988; Rails-to-Trails Conservancy, "27 Million Americans Enjoyed over 200 Rail-Trials in '88," *Trailblazer*, January-March, 1989.

60 **99.** TEST, *Quality Streets.*

100. Michel Labreque, Le Tour de l'Isle, Montreal, private communication July 31, 1989; Alethea Morison, Bicycle Institute of New South Wales, private communication, June 1, 1989.

101. Lapin, "CBS News Sees P.A. as the Bicycle Capital."

102. Melinda Beck, "Smart Cars, Smart Streets."

103. Renner, *Rethinking the Role of the Automobile.*

104. Pucher, "Urban Travel Behavior."

105. Gasoline tax revenues in particular can also support research in automotive fuel efficiency. Potentially regressive effects of increased fuel taxes can be mitigated by a number of direct and indirect measures: low-income drivers can be eligible, for example, for tax coupons presented at the gas pump. Tax revenues can also be used for home weatherization assistance to low-income households and aid in paying heating fuel bills; Nancy Hirsh, Environmental Action Foundation, private communication, July 31, 1989.

106. The author acknowledges that, while the linkages between taxation and auto use are generally clear and consistent, the cause and effect mechanism is more difficult to distinguish, since heavy taxation is politically more feasible in a country in which driving is less important in the first place.

107. Pucher, "Urban Travel Behavior"; Replogle, private communication, August 19, 1989.

108. Erickson, Greene, and Sabadell, "An Analysis of Transportation Energy Conservation Projects in Developing Countries."

109. Replogle, *Bicycles and Public Transportation*; Walter Grabe and Joachim Utech, "The Importance of the Bicycle in Local Public

Passenger Transport: Facts and Experience from Selected Countries," International Commission on Traffic and Urban Planning, *UITP Revue*, March 1984; Werner Brög et al., "Promotion and Planning for Bicycle Transportation: An International Overview," paper presented at the 63rd annual meeting of the Transportation Research Board, Washington, D.C., 1984; Replogle, *Bicycles and Public Transportation*.

110. Bicycle industry examples from Mozer, private communication, August 4, 1989.

111. World Bank, "Sub-Saharan Africa Transport Program: Rural Travel and Transport Project," unpublished draft project proposal, 1989; John D. N. Riverson and Bernard M. Chatelin, World Bank, private communication, February 22, 1989.

112. World Bank, "Sub-Saharan Africa Transport Program."

113. Peter Harnik, *The Bicycle Advocate's Handbook* (Baltimore, Maryland: League of American Wheelmen, 1989).

114. For a thorough guide to safe cycling techniques and other aspects of bicycle transportation, see John Forester, *Effective Cycling* (Cambridge, Mass.: MIT Press, 1984); Carl Hultberg, "Bike/Ped Accidents Drop: Motor Mayhem Continues," *City Cyclist*, March/April 1989; Nadine Brozan, "Bicycle Riding Up; Accidents Decline," *New York Times*, June 10, 1989.

115. Among the many recent publications on urban form and growth management is Madis Pihlak, ed., *The City of the 21st Century*, proceedings of The City of the 21st Century Conference, Tempe, Arizona, April 7–9, 1988.

116. For a comprehensive manual on bicycle advocacy, see Harnik, *The Bicycle Advocate's Handbook*; Clarke, private communication, August 14, 1989.

117. In a meeting with U.S. Transportation Secretary Samuel Skinner,

62 representatives of the League of American Wheelmen also "secured a promise of full consultation in the current development of national transportation policy"; League of American Wheelmen, "Better Bicycling Sought for 120 Million Bicyclists by Year 2000," press release, August 3, 1989.

118. "Argentina: Menem Faces Economic Disaster and Military Intimidation," *Latinamérica Press*, July 6, 1989.

119. McGurn, *On Your Bicycle*.

MARCIA D. LOWE is a researcher at the Worldwatch Institute, where she researches alternatives in agriculture and transportation. She studied French and Political Science at the University of Utah, and holds a master's degree from the University of Pennsylvania in appropriate technology and energy management for development.

THE WORLDWATCH PAPER SERIES

*Those Worldwatch Papers not listed are out of print.

Bulk Copies (any combination of titles)   **Single Copy** $4.00
        2–5: $3.00 each   6–20: $2.00 each   21 or more: $1.00 each

Calendar Year Subscription (1989 subscription begins with Paper 88) U.S. $25.00 __

Make check payable to Worldwatch Institute
1776 Massachusetts Avenue, N.W., Washington, D.C. 20036 USA

Enclosed is my check for U.S. $ _____

_____
name

_____
address

_____
city   **state**   **zip/country**

*Those Worldwatch Papers not listed are out of print.